Selling Your Home For Top Dollar

12 Strategies From A Top Real Estate Team For Getting Your Home Sold Fast At The Best Price

Steve Trang

Selling Your Home For Top Dollar: 12 Strategies From A Top Real Estate Team For Getting Your Home Sold Fast At The Best Price Copyright © 2018 by Steve Trang

All rights reserved. No part of this publication may be reproduced, distributed, or transmitted in any form or by any means, including photocopying, recording, or other electronic or mechanical methods, without the prior written permission of the author, except in the case of brief quotations embodied in critical reviews and certain other noncommercial uses permitted by copyright law.

Jones Media Publishing
10645 N. Tatum Blvd. Ste. 200-166
Phoenix, AZ 85028
www.JonesMediaPublishing.com

Information contained in our published works have been obtained by Jones Media Publishing from sources believed to be reliable from the author. However, Jones Media Publishing does not guarantees the accuracy or completeness of any information published herein and Jones Media Publishing shall not be responsible for any errors, omissions, or claims for damages, including exemplary damages, arising out of use, inability to use, or with regard to the accuracy or sufficiency of the information contained in this publication.

ISBN: 978-1-945849-57-2 paperback
Printed in the United States of America

CONTENTS

Introduction 1

Chapter 1   How To Sell Your Home In The 21st Century 3

Chapter 2   Reputation As The Hiring Criteria For Real Estate Agents. 7

Chapter 3   Listing Your Home 11

Chapter 4   Pricing Is Part Of The 4 Ps 15

Chapter 5   The Power Of Multiple Listing Service (MLS) 19

Chapter 6   Leverage The Power Of Social Media 25

Chapter 7   Getting Value For Your Home Through A Sustainable Selling Strategy 29

Chapter 8   Staging To Sell Your Property. 33

Chapter 9   The Investment And Second Home Seller. 37

Chapter 10   Contracts 43

Chapter 11   Don't Sell Your House More Than Once 49

Chapter 12   Effectiveness Of Internet Based Marketing 57

Chapter 13   Your Next Step 61

About The Author 63

INTRODUCTION

HAVE YOU EVER sold a home before? If you have, then you probably experienced strong bouts of frustration, anger, and disappointment.

If you're like most people, your home is the single largest asset in your life. It is absolutely critical that you sell your home for as much as possible so that you can move on to the next stage of your life with the assets you need.

Additionally, most people say that selling their home was the second most stressful event in their life. Moving was second only to divorce!

By reading this book, two things will happen. First, you will ensure that you'll get the highest purchase price possible, ensuring that you maximize the equity in your home.

Second, you will be better prepared to navigate all of the hassles that comes with selling your home. You'll be aware of all the inconveniences as well as all of the major points in an escrow.

You will learn the top tips and tricks to maximize the price of your home. You will also avoid the key mistakes that many homeowners make when selling their home.

Additionally, you will be better informed when interviewing real estate agents, as the wrong agent will cost you tens of thousands of dollars while wasting your time.

I wrote this book because I'm tired of how our industry treats homeowners. We need to change the home selling experience. I want to remove the stress and make each and every client's experience as positive as possible. Our goal for each client that we serve is that they will be so delighted by our service that they will want to refer their friends and family back to us. One of my favorite quotes is from the great Zig Ziglar.

"You can have everything in life you want, if you will just help enough other people get what they want."

I heard this quote when I first got into real estate, and it has stuck with me throughout my entire career. That is why we've modeled our business after the companies like Nordstrom's, Costco, Southwest Airlines, Ritz Carlton, and Apple.

Selling your home is just one milestone your life's journey. Let's make sure it's a pleasant and enjoyable step!

CHAPTER 1

HOW TO SELL YOUR HOME IN THE 21ST CENTURY

THERE MAY BE many ways to sell a home, but the least stressful is certainly having a real estate agent list it for you on the Multiple Listing Service. The MLS is a system Realtors use to let each other know which homes are available for sale. Through this system, you are able to get the attention of buyers through agents they regularly work with. In addition to having a property on a platform where Realtors constantly search, the information is syndicated to numerous more sites that also attract buyers.

This is just one of the advantages of hiring a Realtor to sell your home. Realtors and agents are professionals with a license to help buy and sell homes in a certain region. They are equipped with legal information and sales tactics that come in handy to facilitate the sale or purchase of properties.

No doubt the home selling process is difficult with so many details to deal with. You need to pack up, ensure that people are doing their jobs all the while trying to manage daily activities. A homeowner must deal with potential buyers, draft contracts and negotiate the deal. This can be quite stressful especially for those who have never sold a home before.

It is therefore helpful to use a real estate agent as the point of contact who will take all the stress away. He/she will negotiate deals and find multiple options that you can compare. Thanks to experience in the trade, a Realtor can easily negotiate the pitfalls, help you deal with the emotional process of selling your home, and even bear most of the liability for the sale. In fact, an agent will help you reduce liability as much as possible.

Time is obviously of the essence as you want to sell your home as fast as possible. Working with an agent is the only way to save time and avoid legal constraints in a home sale gone awry. Agents have vast knowledge of how to value your home and package it in a way that you will sell faster.

That said, it is not mandatory that you use a Realtor to sell a home. As with anything else, it is possible to sell a home on websites, using classified ads, or the old school method of placing a sign in front of a house with contact details for potential buyers to reach you. This seems like a great strategy that will save you money, but is it really? This is such a high-risk tactic that is often compared to self-representation in a court of law.

Choosing to sell your home by yourself only predisposes you to countless liabilities. Make the wise decision and avoid trouble by having a professional oversee the sale of your home.

Trying to sell on your own is akin to telling complete strangers to walk into your home and search through your stuff. You have no way of vetting people who may even pose as legitimate buyers only to endanger your family. If you must allow anyone into your home, make sure they are accompanied by their agent at all times, so you are sure they are genuine. This will help you avoid becoming a victim to thugs who pose as buyers only so they can get an idea of where you hide your valuables.

When you decide to sell a home by yourself, you also carry the burden of writing contracts and disclosures. There are forms available online that you can fill in accordingly, but you must be extremely cautious. If you are unaware of what to disclose and when, then you are in a very risky situation. It is also wise that you know the options at your disposal should things go wrong. Buyers often have professionals looking out for them and sellers need the same. The seller can save themselves a lot of trouble by using a qualified and experienced agent. While selling a home by yourself might save you some money, how much would you stand to lose if you end up in court?

It doesn't make sense to save a few thousands by avoiding agents only to be entangled in legal suits where you will lose more money. Agents know their way around the rules so you are better off working with one so you do not spend time and money trying to figure things out yourself. When looking for a Realtor or real estate agent you should never be in a rush. It is important to vet the company or individual beforehand to ensure that they are reliable and capable of selling your home. Look for agents with a good reputation in your area and make sure they have the right to operate there.

A good real estate agent knows the area, recent home prices, and has the patience to wait until you are satisfied with the options presented. The right real estate agent will indeed ensure a smooth process and the best deal for you no matter which way you decide to sell the property. You will not feel shortchanged, nor will you have to deal with legal battles after the sale of your precious home.

In modern times people are selling their homes on auction sites. eBay allows your agent to list a property even if it is on MLS. Auction sites allow you to promote a property in a different state. They seem most ideal for sellers of vacation homes or those seeking investors. Other auction sites are limited to specific states and most demand that you have more than a single listing.

The danger of using auction sites is that people are often deterred by limited or nonexistent inspection period. Nobody is really willing to spend money on a property without visiting to see its state. Professional home inspection goes beyond the general aesthetics and if left out, you might invest in a property only to realize that it has serious structural damage. If you think this is an ideal way to sell, be sure to consult with your agent who should be familiar with the auction sites in your region.

CHAPTER 2

REPUTATION AS THE HIRING CRITERIA FOR REAL ESTATE AGENTS

THE STRATEGY ON determining which Real Estate Agent to hire depends on a number of factors such as selling a home or buying a home or even both. The National Association of Realtors carried out a study that indicated that 72% of people selling their houses would not hire the services of their previous agent. There are several reasons that are mentioned as being the probable causes for this, but the main reason is poor communication. What is the probable reason for this situation and how can one go about the process of selecting their next ideal real estate agent?

The following are some of the main factors that need to be considered when selecting an effective real estate agent. In the year 2013, the average home seller was approximately 53 years of age and earned a household income of $97,500. In addition, such typical home sellers had resided in their homes for a period of nine years.

Of late, home sellers have been selling their homes for nothing less than 97% of the property's listing price. However, 47% of these sellers reported that they ended up selling their homes at a reduced price compared to the asking price at least one time. A typical home stayed on the market for at least 5 weeks before it was sold off. 39% of home sellers utilized the professional services of a real estate agent that was referred to them by either family or friends. 25% of home sellers hired the same agent that they had worked with previously either to sell a home or even to buy one.

There are several ways individuals can select their next real estate agent effectively. These are getting referrals from relatives or friends, meeting agents at an open house that you attend, using agents who advertise their services in the newspaper, and even using the services of agents who are family or friends due to a feeling of obligation instead of the quality of their service or experience.

Among the ways of finding a real estate agent mentioned above, which is the most effective?

Another factor that people should consider when hiring a quality real estate agent is basing their decision on the individual's reputation. Hiring based on reputation may take one of several forms. It should be noted that the reputation does not necessarily mean the agent who has the largest ad in the daily newspaper. That only implies that the agent has extra money to spend.

It is important to know an agent's track record as well as what other clients have experienced working with the potential agent. The last thing you want is an incompetent real estate agent. The best way to find out what other sellers and buyers think about a certain Realtor or their true track record is by simply asking them. Simply request them to take you through the statistics of the homes that are up for sale in your area, the ones that actually went to sale and the ones that were ultimately sold. Find out the ratio of average list to the sales price and the number of days that the homes on sale remained on the market. Inquire about the track record of your agent compared to the competition to find out if it is worse, better or just similar.

Ask your real estate agent to produce sample testimonials from a few clients so that you can see what other people think about the Realtor. This will allow you to learn if the agent was able to sell the previous client's home within a reasonable period. Furthermore, you will be able to find out if they were able to get their clients an average price for that particular area.

The worst mistake that anyone can make is to hire a real estate agent based on what they promised they could deliver. It is never wise to risk letting your home remain on the market for long periods because of selecting a wrong agent. It is not guaranteed that a home will sell even in a market that is fast paced as every market is quite price sensitive. Most buyers have perform a lot of research online these days, and thus, have adequate information and know the approximate worth of homes.

It is not advisable to hire a real estate agent according to their advertised commission rate as it only leads to disappointment. It is best to hire real estate agents purely based on reputation to avoid frustrations.

CHAPTER 3

LISTING YOUR HOME

SELLING YOUR HOME needs planning. You should use a good strategy that will ensure you to get the highest amount for your house. The strategy should also enable you to sell your home as fast as you want. Setting up the strategy can be taxing, but it's all you need to get the perfect results you want. You need to research other properties for sale in your neighborhood and the different ways people sell their homes. You need someone to help with the selling process, and this requires you to hire a Realtor or an agent. You will need to get your home ready to market to the public, whether it's your family home or an investment property. It's critical to set up a listing to attract the buyer willing to pay the most. The following steps can help you to be able to sell your home faster by listings.

DECIDE ON THE REAL ESTATE AGENT YOU'RE GOING TO HIRE

That requires that you do some quality research so that you can get the best. Get an agent who will sell your house as they promise. It would be advisable to get an agent who has experience in their area of expertise. That is because they will work with the required skills and eventually give you the best outcome. Hiring an experienced agent can be expensive, but it is better than hiring someone poor in the area since this will cost you more in the end.

Design A Marketing Plan

The agent you have should come up with a plan on how to market your home to the public. The agent should be able to understand that different homes are marketed differently and should, therefore, formulate the best plan for your home. That means that the agent should not use a strategy he or she used in another home since they are different. You should get involved with the agent on discussing how you plan to make your home attractive to the public. In case the agent knows any potential buyers or people she knows will be attracted to your property, this will be a good opportunity for you. The agent should then prepare advertisements and sales sheets that will be required for marketing.

These marketing pieces should be eye-catching and interesting enough to catch the attention of potential buyers. It should also make the buyers want to know more about the home by using words that attract attention. The sales sheet should then be distributed to potential clients and all investors in their lists. The agent should be able to have a marketing plan that is affordable and the best approach to make your property known to many. The plan should have a realistic expense.

Carry Out Intense Marketing

The next step is to carry out aggressive marketing to create high demand for your home. You can circulate the sales adverts and sheets to all multiple listing services that you can access. This will increase the number of investors and clients and information about your home and this can lead to an actual client. Your agent can also advertise your home on all the agents' websites, public websites and local newspapers sites.

Make Use Of Signs And Symbols To Advertise Your Home

That is called signage. Make your home attractive to catch the attention of potential buyers. Ensure your signage is setup to draw in buyers who come into your neighborhood looking for homes. Your Realtor should have prominent signage on the lawn and the fence or doors.

The signs should stand out from traditional real estate signs by making offers to potential buyers. These would include, "Buy this House, We'll Buy Yours!" and "Every Day Open House." These help create top of mind consciousness for your home.

You Can Have Your Realtor Guaranteeing The Sale Of Your Home

Some agents may guarantee to buy your home if they don't sell it. They may give you a guaranteed price for your home. In case the buyer has a home they would like to sell, the agent may guarantee to sell their home too if they buy yours. That attracts a larger pool of buyers for your home and may result in a faster sale of your home.

Have Good Quality Pictures Of Your Home.

A picture is worth thousands of words. It's important to have as many photos of your home on the listing as possible. Have bright pictures that show the key aspects of the home to attract buyers. It is advisable to plan for the pictures in your advertisements so that you can incorporate it into your marketing strategy. People tend to forget what they hear more than what they see. The pictures will create a long-lasting effect on the mind of the buyers. That will ensure that potential buyers will call to ask for more information from what they have seen in the pictures.

CREATE UNBELIEVABLE DEMAND

Your agent should demonstrate how they will create that demand. Don't consider the information the agent gives you by word of mouth only. Let them show you from their experience from their past clients. Market your home to buyer's agents. Mostly, the buyer's agents will do the showcasing in your home, not the listing agents. It is a huge a wrong idea that seller's agents will personally bring buyers through the home. It is best to find local brokers and deliver flyers to the agents in that buyer's office. Buyers will trust their agents more than the listing's agents.

CHAPTER 4

PRICING IS PART OF THE 4 PS

SELLING A HOUSE is always a challenging experience. It is a very tough decision, and you will go through a lot of emotions. To others, it is just a simple house. But for you, it is much more than that. You have spent so many years in the house, and there will be plenty of memories attached to the place. However, in these kinds of situations, you can't let emotions sway you. The decisions need to be taken from the head and not from the heart. If you let emotions take control of you, then things will get unnecessarily complicated. You will need to look at your house just like a car or any other thing which you are willing to sell for a price.

When the marketing staff of any big company want to sell a product in the market, their main objective is to get the maximum price for their object and finish the sale as quickly as possible. They consider the 4 P's of marketing which is Product, Price, Place, and Promotion. However, the issue is that most sellers don't pay attention to these 4P's while selling their home. Most people think that all they must do is just hand over their home to some agent, and they will get the best price for the home. However, it doesn't work like that. In order to maximize your bottom line and save time, it is very important to have a well-planned marketing strategy.

And when it comes to selling your home, Price is the most important P. This is the first and the most important criteria which every buyer considers before viewing a potential home. However, it is not easy to determine the perfect price. You will have to do some extensive market research and analyze the market trends and behavioral patterns of the market buyer.

Before selling your house, the first thing which you should do is call your agent and discuss the rates at which similar properties in the neighborhood are selling. You need to compare and find a similar price. There may be different kinds of properties- closed properties and active properties. Closed properties are those which have been already sold. Active properties are those which are currently listed but not yet sold. You should focus more on closed properties because it will give you a better idea. However, you shouldn't ignore the active properties. Comparing also doesn't mean that you blindly copy the rates of your neighboring properties. Your house may be better than your neighbor, but they have listed it at a very high price. If you follow their rate, then you will also end up overpricing your house.

When it comes to pricing, it is also a good idea to look from the viewpoint of an appraiser. An appraiser always looks at the rates at which the similar properties have been sold and makes some adjustments per each situation. For example, if a property having 3 bathrooms was recently sold for $13,0000 and your property has just 2 washrooms, then the appraiser will take that into consideration and fix the price accordingly. However, the appraiser makes clever adjustments and doesn't just blindly add up every dollar. For example, if you invested around $30,000 for your kitchen renovation, then don't expect that you will get $30,000 more than your neighbor's home if the only difference between the two is the kitchen.

While determining the price, appraisers always try to compare with properties lying in the same locality. If a 2 bedroom house with a pool in your neighborhood is valued at $230,000 and a 2 bedroom property without a pool in your neighborhood is valued at $220,000, then it is likely that the value of the pool is around $10,000. However, it is important to compare properties in the same locality. The prices of properties will vary based on location.

Sometimes you will often find that people do not do any market research for determining the price, and they will just come up with a price in their head with no calculation whatsoever. They are willing to wait until they get the price they are looking for. This is probably the worst possible idea. This way, your house will remain unsold for a long period of time. And in case your house remains listed for a long time, no one will be willing to buy the house anymore.

Just take a look at this example to get a clearer idea. You are visiting a car lot. There are three exactly identical cars in the lot. The price of two of them is $30000 and the price of the third one is $35000. Every time a car worth $30000 is being sold, it is replaced by another one. Since they are identical, no one is going to buy the one worth $35000. That car will stay in the lot for a long period of time. Even if there is nothing wrong with the car, people will think that there are some issues, and that is why no one is buying it. This is why you should always keep a tab on the current market trends. If you find that nobody is interested in buying your house, then you should probably lower the price a bit.

Before you start the selling process, you should set some goals in advance. After that, you have to decide your strategies based on the achievement of your goals. It is the job of your agent to collect all the relevant data related to your neighborhood and come up with a solution to meet the goals. In case you are not able to achieve the predetermined targets, you may need a change in strategy.

There are several ways to increase the traffic to your house. The most obvious way is to make some changes in the price of the house. However, price doesn't just mean list price. There are other ways as well. For example, you may increase the commission of your agent or you may decide to pay the closing cost on behalf of the buyer. Increasing the commission of the agent definitely helps. There have been several instances where an agent has been able to find a buyer just after his commission was raised.

Although it isn't supposed to work like that; agents should work hard regardless whether there is any business or not. However, it is a normal human tendency to work harder in case there is some extra motivation. There are several other tricks as well. For example, you may agree to pay some costs on behalf of your buyer. If you agree to pay the home warranty or some allowance for painting, then you may see a sudden surge in traffic.

In case you make some changes in your strategy, it is very important to know how the market is seeing the change. There are several metrics available which you can use to find out how many people are exactly viewing your property. Just call your agent and he will be able to give you all the relevant information. You will get to know how many people are viewing your strategies online and what are the various activities taken by them. All these will help you to know where you exactly stand and what changes you need to make. For example, if you find out that around 1000 people are viewing your property online and only 1 or 2 of them are actually showing up to your house, then there must be something wrong with your picture. You need to immediately make some changes. You should have frequent conversations with your agent. He will be able to tell you about the different metrics and where you are lacking. Depending on the metrics, you will need to adjust your strategy. The strategy should be flexible.

CHAPTER 5

THE POWER OF MULTIPLE LISTING SERVICE (MLS)

THIS INFORMATION AGE has introduced an unparalleled rate of development in every kind of information and technology. The development of technologies like the internet together with smart phones has totally changed the manner in which people look for and sell their properties. A joint study conducted by The National Association of Realtors and Google reveals that over 90% of people start off their home searches on the internet. Therefore, the internet has revolutionized the manner in which buyers search and Realtors sell properties. This section will address the different ways through which you can use to promote your home for sale via the internet.

In 2014, Trulia was acquired by the real estate aggregation giant Zillow. This acquisition makes Zillow the biggest online home sales presence. Though each site keeps on to operating independently, the acquisition prompted several months of discussions on the prospect of home sales. Well, being a real estate expert with more than a decade of experience and being an optimist and have invested a greater part of my adult life on the internet, I have also followed this pattern with great enthusiasm.

To start with, let us observe the order of actions which many homes follow to get posted on a website like Zillow. With respect to this discussion, I will restrict my observations to Zillow since it is considered the most popular realty website on the net. The regular order of events starts with a property seller getting in touch with a Realtor who then get their home listed on the Multiple Listing System (MLS) of that locality. The systems are regulated by the local council of Realtors and published on the MLS.

As soon as it is published on the MLS, the property is then advertised to other Realtors in that location who may have potential buyers searching for a property that is much like the one recently posted. Prior to the advent of internet, everything will simply stop at this point because local real estate brokers were the only people with complete access to details on every single property posted for sale in the locality and buyers would talk with agents to understand more about what properties could be for sale that suits their particular tastes. Listings usually emerge through a periodic MLS book, and hot sheets were utilized for spreading information like price modifications and so on.

Now with the advent of internet, the listings are organized by local property brokerages and offer to firms such as Zillow to post on their site. There is a little hindrance in this process, and it is not the whole information that is relevant to the listing is supplied to Zillow. However, the major attributes and advantages of the property together with its images are generally made available. It's essential to remember that Zillow was created to be a consumer website. It is simple and pleasurable to see and displays people what they have an interest in seeing. In contrast, The MLS was created to be agent inclined and is develop with the expert real estate agent in mind.

Its power is substantially bigger on the Realtor side, and there are countless ways for agents to make use of the MLS to explore properties in ways Zillow cannot compete with. As soon as a property listing gets to Zillow, it will be available for entire world to view, accordingly increasing the listing's reach. Though Zillow and other similar websites are fantastic resources for property buyers, the sellers and the people who simply take pleasure in viewing properties , every bit of the information disseminated about it should not been taken at face value and a real estate agent must be contacted for further information .

As stated earlier, this is how most of the properties are published on Zillow. Individuals wishing to promote their property as For Sale by Owner (FSBO) are also allowed to list their own property on Zillow at no cost and need not engage a real estate agent anymore. This leads to the question, "does a property seller have to employ a real estate agent to sell off their property or is posting it on Zillow on their own really that good?"

In the meantime, we will set aside the many advantages that accompany having the support of someone who has made it his only profession to market properties and consider the advertising side. Recently, an experiment was conducted to assess the marketing potential of Zillow.

In January of 2014, an agent decided to sell his property in Scottsdale, Arizona. The first thing he did was to list the home on Zillow for two weeks. After these two weeks he switched to posting the home in the MLS. He engaged an expert photographer and had him photograph the property.

Thereafter, he had it listed on Zillow and linked it to every other leading real estate website. For the two weeks the property was listed on Zillow, he received four calls altogether without any showings and zero offers. After the two weeks, he posted the same property on the MLS using the same description, images and asking price as on Zillow. Within a week, he received 4 offers and had 13 showings. Out of those offers, two were even above asking price. In the end, he sold for $12,000 above asking price, and the deal was closed just 3 weeks after.

This basic minor experiment is a great illustration of the marketing potential of a system such as your local MLS even more essential the real estate agents that sign up for it. To assist you figure out why there is that a big difference in the results achieved we need to begin from a fundamental insight into how Zillow gets its money, and also how Realtors use Zillow. Zillow is completely free to the buyer, and its sole revenue source is from advertisers, and Realtors constitute a larger percentage of these advertisers.

At a price, Realtors can use Zillow to promote their services with the anticipation that buyers will get in touch with them whenever they are prepared to buy or sell a property. Zillow does not have any motivation to assist getting your property sold. The only thing they are interested in is getting website visitors and getting that site visitors comes directly from one of their paying clients, i .e. real estate agent. Conversely, agents only earn money if they actually make a sale. Zillow is interested in advertisers, and Realtors are interested in getting a client's properties sold. Their incentives or motivation are totally different just like the results.

This system depends on the notion that many of us would prefer to make the greatest financial decision of our lives without the assistance of an expert. This notion has been disproven over and over again. With the internet increasing in its reach, numerous uniform fee brokerages including firms like Redfin were established. These firms are discount brokerages and have a rather narrow service that premise their business ideas on the notion that consumers would prefer to save money instead of having a full time Realtor. Time has proven that customers always get whatever they pay for. Moreover, many of these firms have either closed down or still pushing on with little motivation left. This model is defective. As with any sector, the best individuals in the real estate industry will be attracted to bigger paying full time business models and those that have the lowest experience and competence will be attracted to business built around cheaper costs.

The finest agents have accepted these new marketing mediums and perform extraordinarily well promoting their customer's homes online. In this information age, people wish to carry out some fundamental investigation by themselves, particularly at the start of their findings and when they become serious they love to have the services of dependable expert who sells houses every day. This is now the reality with agents. For example, Google any agent you're interviewing, and you will potentially find them on numerous sites. Home buyers no longer find out about the home they are keen on buying, but they depend on the real estate agent to do this on their behalf. Ultimately, this accessibility of information is greatly important to property buyers and sellers and will ensure that they have better agents to render services to them.

The truth remains that there is no replacement for the incredible marketing potential of a local full time real estate agent when you make use of your local MLS. As the saying goes, you ALWAYS get what you pay for.

CHAPTER 6

LEVERAGE THE POWER OF SOCIAL MEDIA

MERRIAM WEBSTER DICTIONARY describes social media as the forms of electronic communication through which the users create communities online where they share ideas, information, messages and other digital content such as videos and images. Social media websites which can give online presence easily include LinkedIn, Facebook, Twitter, Instagram, Picasa, YouTube, Reddit, Pinterest, Google+, Photobucket, Flickr, Foursquare and much more. There is no payment that you need to make to create a profile on these websites although some, such as LinkedIn, have premium membership level at a certain minimum cost per month.

Let us go back to the year 2000. The social media concept back then meant marketing to your own social circle either by passing or word of mouth advertising, that is, to your circle of friends. During this period Facebook was not the main media social networking site like it is today. Pinterest and Instagram were not in existence and Google+ was just an idea by that time. To get a message across thousands or hundreds of thousands of people costs a lot of money. During the early 2000s, a typical real estate agent was depending on printed ads or direct mail to advertise and expose homes that were available for sale to the mass public.

Someone who claimed to enjoy social media presence during this period, it usually meant that you had a MySpace account, which had testimonials from the sphere that you influence, or you have some type of blog, either power by blogger or Xanga (blogpost.com).

Fast forward to today. You find that almost every real estate agent knows the social media power, and they use it to advertise the products that they are selling on a daily basis. Even the least savvy real estate agents own a personal Facebook profile while most make use of the business profile. My real estate staff and I personally make use of Facebook to not only reach and connect with our clients but also to spread and expose our brand to the mass public.

Rather than depending solely on the direct mailing method to get our advertising and marketing message spread around to our target audience, I also make use of the social media sites to get my message across the masses effectively and quickly. I can post a single image of the house that I am selling on Facebook for instance and send it along with a catchy headline that speaks directly to the buyers. That single photo will be accessed and seen by my network of friends and my friend's network of friends as well. The more likes that you get on your Facebook posts or images, the more network of friends you can be able to infiltrate. You never know if one of your friends on your network is looking for a house to buy in your neighborhood. Better yet, you can't tell if they are looking for a home that is exactly just like yours.

As a real estate team, we generate interest from hundreds of people who are looking for a home to buy each year through our social media marketing, and each year many home buyers who we found using our proven marketing system end up purchasing a home with us in future. My real estate team of staff is proof that social media marketing works. Did I mention at the beginning that social media is absolutely free? You can get your message around to a huge number of people a very fast way without paying any cost!

Now, what happens in case you have a small network of friends? More so, what if you can't get your friends to like, or comment on your posts? What if you don't have enough time to wait for your Facebook post or images to go viral? Well, here are the secrets on how I get my Facebook posts on the top of everyone else's newsfeed. Simple, I opt to pay for it. I have found out that Facebook Ads are one of the greatest ways to spread a message online faster to the target audience.

For instance, with a mere $25 I can expose and showcase a new home available for sale to a super targeted audience, which is over 7,000 people. Facebook gives me the ability to target the audience I want by occupation, age, interest, education level, spending habits, location, ownership, etc. Make the comparison of this method to the direct mail. A typical direct mail postcard alone can cost you about $0.34 per piece that was back in 2014. If you happen to send 7,000 postcards, the postage alone will cost you about $2,380, that doesn't have the cost of printing the postcards, or to buy the targeted mailing list.

The amount of money that we spend on Facebook varies depending on the property and targeted buyer. It's not unusual for us to spend upward of $1000 to get the proper reach for our listings.

A MESSAGE OR AN OFFER FOR YOUR AUDIENCE

A common posting would be to promote an open house or a coming soon listing. It could be just a listed blast to friends. In order to ensure that your message is outstanding, we ensure it speaks to the target audience directly. We use a high definition attention-grabbing photo if the ad t is meant to sell a house. The best photo is either the house front's, the family room or the kitchen room.

A Defined Audience

I know for sure this might sound silly but it is very important to be clear on who you are trying to reach. This is in regards to your house selling, is it an ideal move up buyer you are targeting or is it a first time home buyer? We need to cater the ad copy to our targeted audience.

A Landing Page

A landing page is a website or a webpage where your audience arrives when they click on your ad. This page should sound and needs to look like your ad. We use the same theme and color scheme. Use similar fonts as well. This page should reiterate the message you have put on your Facebook ad. The main purpose of the landing page is to capture the audience's contact information.

A Call to Action

A call to action simply tells the audience what to do so that they can obtain the information that you are offering. Some of the best call to actions messages that we use include call Steve at #### - ####### for a no-obligation consultation or visit www.searchphoenixhomes.com to get the latest up to date homes for sale. Be concise and specific in your call to action message.

Performance Tracking

We track engagement on our ads. The reason that's important to you, the home seller, is that we know how to effectively target the ideal buyer for your home. By using proven ad-copy, style, and photography, we have a much greater chance of finding the buyer for you!

Chapter 7

Getting Value For Your Home Through A Sustainable Selling Strategy

ONE OF THE most important milestones you will achieve in life will be selling your home. You gave it a lot of thought prior to purchasing it, and now that you want to sell an asset near and dear to your heart, you expect to achieve nothing short of meaningful monetary gains.

The National Association of Realtors expresses that a high percentage of people surveyed who sold their homes as a For Sale By Owner say they would rather not use that approach again. The justification being challenges such as determining the price, marketing difficulties, limited time and liability issues. If you choose to seek a Realtor, vet about two or three. Carefully assess quotes that are overly low or overly high.

Realtors are different. A professional Realtor has adequate knowledge with respect to the market, recent listings, effective marketing strategies and detailed information on past sales. Further, he will divulge more information about his area of specialization and offer references to enable you to evaluate his credibility. Be sure to assess every Realtor to confirm their suitability using qualifiers such as skills, level of experience, and personal character in order to select the most qualified person.

If you prefer to sell independently, there is no harm in talking to a Realtor. Most Realtors are always ready to support do-it-your-selfers to sail through the entire process smoothly. A Realtor will come in handy when you need assistance with respect to paperwork and contracts.

Appearance Is Your Greatest Cutting Edge

The appearance of your home bears an impact on the selling process. The greatest emotional response is triggered through the appearance projected by your home. Potential buyers are more interested in the things in your home as opposed to the selling price. The smell, what they see or hear influences their buying decisions.

Do not give in to the temptation to install old fashioned for sale signs. Focus on creating an appealing and large for sale sign that will woo prospective buyers. There are high chances that your big FOR SALE sign will motivate prospective buyers to spare a few minutes to gather some information about your home.

Engage In Cleaning And Repair/Renovations

Prospective buyers are normally wooed by homes that are clean, tidy and in great condition. Invest in improving the condition of your home by eliminating dirt, clutter and conducting repairs where necessary. A simple thing such as a dysfunctional light switch or a cracked mirror in the bathroom can put off a potential buyer. Do not forget there are other homeowners who are out to sell their homes just like you and brand new homes yearning to be occupied as well.

Let Potential Buyers Feel Welcomed In Your Home

You surely do not want to display a home characterized by clutter thus making potential buyers feel like strangers and unwelcomed in your home. Minimize clutter, personal documents and keep your closets tidy. Choose appealing colors - white or beige - and items that enhance the décor, elegance and warmth of your home. Place vase of flowers in suitable spaces such as the bathroom. To get it all right when it comes to decorating your home, use home décor-magazines to acquire useful tips.

Do Not Ignore The Input Of Interior Designers

A qualified interior designer and team can give your home the transformation it needs to suit the needs of potential buyers through home staging. Incorporation of new custom furniture, quality and right lighting, color combination, patterns, organization by the interior designer not only gives your home an aesthetic touch, but also enhances its overall outlook.

Only showcase your home to potential buyers when you are certain your home is ready. To determine how ready your home is for showcasing, use the four Cs.

Clean. Nothing should be left to chance. Every corner of your home and all the things in your home must be spotless clean to give your home a brand new look.

Clutter-free. Keep your home organized and neat to allow potential buyers judge if the house has enough space instead of shifting their attention to your personal items.

Color. Neutral colors give potential buyers hope that their furniture can blend in well.

Creativity. A long lasting and great impression of the home should be printed on the minds of buyers even after they view other homes through everything in it.

No odors please!

Creative. The way you layout your furniture can make a significant impression on potential home buyers. You can help them see your home as more spacious and where the furniture belongs.

It may seem like a simple issue, but it is very critical. Weird odors from pets, smoking odors, spoilt food- can discourage potential buyers. It is likely prospective buyers will quickly become very sensitive to every little smell and even imagine odors that hardly exist. Ensure your home is devoid of odors that may compromise selling your house.

Get as many offers as you can

If you conduct a serious marketing campaign for your home, you will get the attention of several prospective buyers. The good thing about getting multiple offers is that buyers strive to outdo each other as opposed to a case where only one buyer exists who only competes with you.

Chapter 8

Staging To Sell Your Property

WHEN STAGING TO sell your property, you should prepare by de-cluttering and pre-pack your belongings. The tidiness and orderliness of your house will appeal to most potential buyers in the market. There are things that you need to think of such as how spacious your house feels, the look of your garage, how clean your house is, and the look of an area of your house that maybe was unfinished and used it for storage. Prepack all unnecessary items when you have your home for sale and decide on a place for storage.

The front yard, backyard, and side yard should also be appealing. An attractive exterior will create a lasting impression on the buyer. He or she will be anxious to stop to view your home's interior if it's well maintained in the interior and exterior and looks well cared for. Just take in what major and minor repairs are required. You will need to get walkways, driveways, and deck swept or shoveled. Place flowers or winter arrangements on your front porch. Maintain the curb clean and beautiful.

Depersonalization is a crucial step when selling your home. This process can be tough, but you have to let go emotionally. Upon deciding to sell your house, it is time to move you need to remove your identity from the house. By disconnecting yourself from the house, potential buyers can emotionally connect with living there rather than feeling like guests. You will need to store personal and family photos away. Remove all memorabilia topper-pack books, kids toys, and games that aren't appealing to most buyers. If you have any belongings that can potentially discourage buyers such as animal trophies, you'd instead put them off.

Your house's flooring is as well a vital part of home sale preparedness. The buyers want a home ready for move in. A top-selling feature that clients consider when buying a home is up to date flooring. You need to look at the condition, color, and the style of your carpet. You need to think in case the carpet needs replacing, should it be in every room? If not, you should select something that will do with the rest of the carpeting in the house. You need to consider the style of vinyl flooring you have and need for replacement. If you have hardwood, you should find out whether it needs refinishing.

Proper furniture placement will display a room to its full potential. Keep in mind buyers will walk through each room, if you have excessive furniture that clutters and makes a room seem small, then you should consider putting it in storage while your home is on the market. Lighting is also a key factor for making a good impression. Make sure to have all lights on for pictures and showings. When your furniture and lighting are appropriately placed, they will allow buyers to see the function of each room and principal features. You need to think about how much furniture is in each room, how it is placed, its size and condition. You may consider purchasing or renting new furniture. You need to know the amount of light in each room and the state of permanent light fixtures.

A home inspection is crucial before it is listed. An inspection will determine whether any significant repairs are needed, and they can be worked on before the house goes on the market for sale. A real estate agent can recommend you the right home inspector. When the inspection is complete, you can decide what the next steps are in preparing your home for sale. You should think about the age of your house and the condition of your foundation. You should check your lights flicker, breakers, and blown fuses. You also need to check the state of your plumbing. Make sure your windows are in excellent condition. Consider resolving if you have water problems if you have had issues with mold and mildew. Consider the status of your roof and how old your furnace is.

You should pay considerable attention to the main selling rooms. The overall impression of your whole home is essential. Potential buyers will focus on the main selling rooms such as the front entrance, living area, and kitchen. You need to think about the front porch and how the rooms look from the spot you are standing. You should consider whether your entrance feels spacious.

Take in how the kitchen looks and feels when you walk into it. Identify the areas that need change. Also, consider the look of your pantry. Make your living room feel warm and inviting. Consider the arrangement of your furniture and any repairs or upgrades that needs doing. For the master bedroom, family room and dining room, consider if each of them shows its function the arrangement of its furniture and any repairs and upgrades that are needed.

AIR QUALITY/ODOR/PETS/HOLIDAYS

Most people overlook air quality and smell, but these are essential parts of home selling preparedness as well. Buyers want to envision themselves living in the house. An overpowering odor can deter them from wanting to see the house. Pets with dirty litter boxes or uncleaned yard space with animal waste can be a deal killer. Not everyone loves pets, and some have allergies which could be a concern if they are potentially interested in purchasing your home. You should think about the year your house was constructed. As well what time of the year you are selling, and if there is going to be any holidays during that time.

If you have had any water issues, check for mold and mildew. It is crucial to inspect your smoke and carbon monoxide detectors and replace the defective ones. Avoid cooking with strong seasonings and foods with lingering aromas. Remove your pets and all their signs while your house is on the market. You should hide them during showings if they must stay in the house and keep litter boxes clean and out of sight.

The paint of your house is essential. If your house is bright or has unusual colors, potential buyers will be turned off or even negotiate too low your asking price. Neutral colors are warm for the eye. Buyers also want to stay in a house for long before deciding to repaint the house. Think of the last time you painted your house and whether you have a warm color palate and whether your walls need a neutral color paint. If they already are neutral, do they need a fresh coat of paint? It's great if you have a wallpaper too. Check if your doors need a fresh paint coat. A new coat of paint on the ceiling will give a clean look to the entire room.

Look out for updates and repairs. An objective look at your house determines the necessary maintenance and upgrades. Based on your budget and timeline, you should identify and do things that should be done to improve the overall presentation of your home. Buyers are willing to pay more for a well-maintained house so show them your home is in absolutely perfect condition. You need to think of your timeline and budget, updates and repairs required, state of your doors and trim and holes or cracks in your walls.

Chapter 9

The Investment And Second Home Seller

THIS CHAPTER IS meant to help the investors and the corporations by giving them an insight on matters which need appropriate measures to be taken. This section also guides those in need of a home mortgage. The following information is just as essential for a corporate buyer or an acquisition manager as it guides you through the unexpected and the problems experienced and how to overcome them.

How is your Property Insured?

When the new owners and corporations are buying, the kind of transaction determines the insurance policy. The kind of home you purchase does not guarantee you excellent coverage. Ensure the coverage is genuine to help out in case something happens to your home.

Home Owner Associations (HOAs)

The HOA is known with various names depending on your area of residence, but it serves the same purpose. They are spread countrywide to help in the development and improving the conditions. If not well examined, HOAs can cause serious harm to investors and owners during the transaction. That can happen when a corporation buys a home without following the actual procedures of acquiring a title, accompanied by debt in HOA. Nowadays HOAs are doing business with the foreclosures. Some collection companies and HOA management firms are not to be trusted as they exaggerate from what is in statements. When acquiring a home, contact the real estate division's to guide on the HOA which is under the law. The home exterior will require more maintenance if your area has a strict HOA management.

In some cases, the corporate sellers poorly estimate the value required by their homes after the tenants who have been servicing and maintaining the property. After the foreclosure, the home is placed on the market, and immediately the fines from HOA starts coming in and sometimes causing the violation. This attracts unforeseen expenses which are reflected on your closing statement and cannot be avoided. If the HOA in your area is strict, you will be subjected to more maintenance on your home exterior. Have this in mind when makes plans for marketing your home.

CASH FOR KEYS AGREEMENT: DEALING WITH UNWANTED OCCUPANTS.

In some cases, an investor buys a home with people are living here unlawfully. The investor has two options, either goodwill or forceful evacuation. Earlier communication to the occupants about the evacuation is recommendable for them.

An honest agreement termed as Cash for Keys agreement is signed by the owner and the occupant. It gives the dates on which the occupants should move out of the home. For its success, the occupant should leave home intact. It reduces the investor's payouts required to move the occupants. The payout value is determined by the value of the assets and the timeline set for the occupant to move.

It is necessary for an investor to note the typical eviction schedule when buying a home which will later be put back to the market.

Useful and Frequently Occurring Services

Utilities should not be left off on homes as this breaks some of the HOA rules and it endangers plants life. Also, it delays the services of those working in your home and the sellers.

During the winter season, use less power to warm your home so that the pipes will not freeze and cause damages. Also winterizing is vital to help have moderate climate condition. This entails the shutting down of all the plumbing and vacuums the lines. In case of electrical dangers, the power should remain off unless the master breaker is off. When an investor acquires a new home, they should ensure that the water master line is off before turning on the water to be used at home.

When an Action to Repair Is Required

When marketing the acquired home; three main points need to be considered before fixing. These are; the market trends at that particular time; before repairing the home, the seller should find out if the market is favorable for quick sales or extended periods for buyers to purchase.

The quick market requires less or no repairs, unlike a slower market where a home needs to be repaired to attract the buyers.

Kind of likely highest bidder; VA or FHA buyers tend to access your home, take safety measures and need for maintenance. These end up causing delays if not taken care of in time. One can get these kinds of mortgages with an old and unrepaired home. What you need to do is to repair your home within the stipulated period.

Home with a vandalism trend; repairs are not necessary to a home which is likely to be always vandalized. The house remains vacant waiting to be purchased, while it is being repainted or maintained.

Using Data and Accessing the Home Market

A home with tenants needs more strategies, and when one intends to sell it, can be delayed due to procedures. For a cyclical seller markets, it's relevant to the time when homes are occupied easily. For example, Phoenix is busiest from February until the end of July. Access the data from the professionals to study the data trends on various seasons.

A Home with a Dog

The Dog is an excellent example of what makes it hard to sell a home. You don't have to ignore it when setting the home value. Include to the price of other properties that make your asset to be of higher quality compared to the neighboring sales. Price your property reasonably otherwise investors will choose those high expectations that are accompanied by price set.

Consider the surroundings, in case of a busy street, get something like a pool of water or play some jazz with a wireless jam box for a calm environment. If you are dealing with odors in the home, do not make the mistake of just changing out the flooring and not treating the area underneath. Employ contractors to change the carpet and handle underneath to eliminate the odor of all kinds.

Good Standards for Vacant Homes

The hired agent is supposed to check your vacant home weekly. This helps to minimize various problems. In case of unexpected occurrence and you file the claim. The insurance company can get the recent reports from your agents to show when the issue arose.

Employ vendors to ensure your home is cleaned inside, and lawn maintained to keep it appealing to potential buyers. These vendors keep an eye on the property and inform you of any issues that arise.

MAKING USE OF CODE ENFORCEMENT

Code enforcement is essential to help watch for uncontrollable landscaping, pools changing from blue to green and wreckage in the yard. An old and falling over home attracts vast fines or complete destroying of the home. It is necessary to contact them to take care of these concerns with immediate effect.

REDUCING THEFT RISKS

Theft is an issue of great concern to the investors as their homes are not occupied, and the property isn't taken care of. The type of thefts may include; that of significant appliances, roof mounted AC units, pool pumps and copper piping in the walls.

Some individuals have mastered various tricks to keep their properties safe from the thieves. Such as: securing the garage doors and side gates with a padlock; this is because the garage door is a passage of removing permanent appliances out of the home. Lock the garage door and remove the opener while in its empty state. The side gates serve as alternative exits. Therefore, they should be as well locked.

Make use of the signage as much as you can. The signs help your Vacant home to be noticed by curious neighbors. It will be of much assistance as they will be vigilantes to your home and informs you when things are not in excellent condition. Share your contacts with them and make sure you place a sales sign close to their homes.

Use of Theft deters stickers. They are usually put on good looking appliances. The stickers have a police badge on them and appear similar to the ones the Government issues with warning labels. They show that GPS tracker can track each object. They are mainly used for significant appliances and pool equipment.

Have a meaningful name and number Printed on the exterior part of the equipment. This prevents the theft of Pool pumps and other exterior housing appliances. Through writing your names, phone number and symbolic surname on equipment will help deter the vandalism.

Chapter 10

Contracts

Wikipedia defines a contract in the following way:

IN MOST COMMON law legal jurisdictions, a contract (or agreement) is a pact or agreement that entails a lawful object that is voluntarily entered into by two or more parties, with each of them intending and agreeing to the creation of one or more legal obligations between the parties. The elements of a contract include offer and acceptance by competent persons with legal capacity who in their agreement exchange consideration to ensure mutuality of obligation.

Breaking this down into layman's language: a contract is something agreed upon by two or more people with each person gaining something as well as giving up something more in return, and is legally enforceable.

The definition above is much easier to swallow than the heavy jargon and wordy legalese taught at law school. Indeed, this seems to be intentionally the case to confuse the general public so that people rely on the law community.

To people like Frederick Sawyer, a contract is a pact that is binding on the weaker party!

In one case study, Lucy v. Zehmer, two parties met in a bar and discussed the purchase and sale of a farm worth $50,000. The figure was much lower than the property's true value. They finally came to an agreement on the price, recorded it on a bar napkin and each party signed.

Initially, it would appear that this contract can't be legally enforceable because a "real" contract must be on a "government-blessed", magically-rendered contractual document to be considered legal. Long story short, without boring you with all the nitty-gritties on the legal elements involved in that particular case, in the end it was not only legal but also an enforceable contract.

I am sure you are wondering how a bar napkin can be legally enforceable. In practice, you may decide to paint your contract on one side of a cow but as long as all its legal elements have been met, then it is enforceable!

This being a real estate book, it is crucial that all the information here loops back to the real estate process. One day, you are going to have your real estate transaction at the contractual phase. One question that is seldom asked by both buyers and sellers is how well one understands the process involved in this phase?

Typically, people will ask the following questions:

— How many pieces of property did you sell this year?

— How many buyers do you are you currently working with?

— What kind of marketing do you provide in your company?

— What is your commission structure?

Quite shockingly, the most critical element of the contractual phase of real estate is what is rarely discussed. Next time you interact with a real estate professional, ask them if they have any contractual strategies that go beyond what an agent would typically provide. While any professionally-competent agent will be able to fill in the blanks on a standard purchase contract, an elite agent should be able to offer you some competitive contractual advantages since they are representing your interests.

A basic discussion we often have with our clients up front is that a contract could be any pact that two parties are willing to come to an agreement on.

Below is the example we love to use to ensure our clients think outside the box:

> Us: Mr. Buyer, are you aware that there is a Miscellaneous section in this contract where I can add anything I want to this contract?
>
> Buyer: No, I did not know about that.
>
> Us: Actually, there is. For instance, I can write in there that you have agreed to pay the full price for this home as long as the seller comes back every other Thursday to wash your car for the next six months!
>
> Buyer: That sounds a bit ridiculous and possibly can't be enforceable!
>
> Us: As long as you both agree to such an arrangement, and sign the contract, it is not ridiculous at all. In fact, that way it becomes an enforceable element of your contract.

If a client begins to perceive the contractual process as something more than the ink that is used to pen it on paper, it opens up a whole world of possibilities to aid in putting deals together that may otherwise never have the chance to see light of day.

For example, imagine you are working with a client who does not have lots of cash to work with such that they cannot afford an initial property deposit of $1,000 to $10,000. Most agents would right at that point be dead in the water.

But did you know that there is no requirement for the initial deposit to be in cash? For a contract to be legal, all it needs is an initial deposit (or consideration) that is something of value. For instance, a creative contract could be worded like below:

"John Smith offers to buy your property for $100,000. He will make one initial deposit of $100 and then hand over the title to his 2007 Nissan Sentra valued at $5,000. The seller will then carry back the balance of $94,900, with payments to be made monthly at..." So long as the seller and the buyer agree to the particular terms in their agreement, a legal contract is created.

BUYERS

Never be afraid to get creative and powerful with your offers. In case you are in a competitive situation and you find yourself offering your absolute maximum, and as far as that is what you financially qualify for, you can have your agent throw in something that your life skills are able to offer.

* If you are a mechanic for instance, why not offer free oil changes for six months?

* And if you are a baker, why not offer free pies once per week for the next year?

Do something that may not cost you a whole lot while simultaneously offering perceived value that raises the worth or strength of your offer, and also makes it a bit more unique compared to your competitors' black and white offers.

Indeed, you may be inclined to say: I have the most boring job ever known to man. It offers no goods, services or anything else of value to the general population. I am sorry. But I still have some quite viable solution for you: I will buy a whole year's tickets to Disneyland!

Consider the kind of psychological effect this kind of proposition has when your offer gets presented side by side to a competitor's basic vanilla contract.

In a highly-competitive market like Phoenix, in my experience such propositions have had a tremendous impact. Such little, creative elements are capable of leading you to contract victory. Although it may be impossible to be an expert at contracts by just reading a few short pages like this on such a deep topic, my hope is that I have challenged your perspectives on what a contract actually is, and what it can be.

CHAPTER 11

DON'T SELL YOUR HOUSE MORE THAN ONCE

HAS YOUR HOUSE been for sale for just a week, but it feels like years of waiting and then your real estate agent calls! You answer excitedly hoping that this is the D-day. After the numerous daily visits by potential buyers for an entire week, could this be the first offer you received? As you answer the phone, your agent's voice seems unusually excited and positive. Mr. Jefferson, I couldn't wait to tell you the superb news, I have received a full price offer on your house!

Full of excitement, you start jumping up and down celebrating. You hug and kiss your wife exclaiming, we got a great deal honey, we are rich! You will now be able to purchase that new house you have been chasing on the other side of the city! Just as you are beginning to congratulate him and promise a token for the wonderful job, he cautions you. Mr. Jefferson let's not be too excited yet! Although this is an amazing first step, we are just beginning. The buyer is highly motivated to buy your home, but before the deal is finalized we have to brace ourselves for some challenges. Could you please calm down so that I can take you through the next few steps?

As usual, the first offer elucidates a lot of excitement to sellers. Unfortunately, many real estate contracts fall apart before they are finalized and as a seller, you are forced back to square one. The cycle begins again as you start the process of showing and waiting for buyers once more hoping to make a successful sale soon. This chapter will help you prevent these challenges and guarantee that the first offer you accept closes successfully!

Remember Who's in Charge

As the seller, it is critical to remember that many purchase contracts are formulated to provide buyers with a number of ways out of the contract and sellers only get very limited ways out. This is because buyers assume all the risks related to making a big purchase. Given that you have limited ways out and buyers have numerous ways out, as a seller you should be selective about the buyers whose offers you accept. To ensure a buyer who signed the contract doesn't cancel later, you will have to address three main issues before every offer which are; buyer motivation, access to financing and potential contractual challenges.

Buyer Motivation

How desperate is the buyer to purchase your home? This is probably the most critical question to ask. As a seller, you desire a buyer who will go all in to ensure they purchase your house! In the real estate industry, this means a buyer who has an actual and serious need to purchase and has definite reasons why your house is perfect for them. Ask your agent to conduct further inquiries on these questions with the buyer's agent.

You may encounter less motivated investors who hope to make your home a rental. In competitive markets, investors will submit offers in advance and end up canceling after viewing the house. You need a buyer who takes time to view the home, take pictures, and measurements. You need a family that visited and deliberated that this is their perfect home; they really need to buy your home!

I have definitely created exciting images, but in reality, not all homes will produce the high levels of inspiration described here. Homes that are overpriced, in unfavorable neighborhoods, or in need of total remodeling will get few or no offers and you may be forced to sell at what is offered in some cases. Nonetheless, you will need to effectively gauge the excitement level of your potential home buyers at all times.

Below are some questions to help you ascertain whether your buyer is interested:

- Has the buyer viewed the home previously and if so how many times?

- For how long did the buyer view the home previously?

- What was the buyer's excitement after viewing your home on a scale of 1-10?

- Has the buyer previously entered into a contract with other home sellers and canceled later? This is a crucial question to assist you to discover buyers who tend to withdraw from contracts during escrow.

- How long has the buyer's agent known the buyers? A prolonged relationship will translate to highly valuable information about his/her clients.

- How many homes has the agent sold this year? A reliable and energetic agent will be time conscious and will only bring you highly motivated buyers.

CONTRACTUAL CONTINGENCIES

Every purchase contract contains several ways by which the buyer can exit the deal. Such exits are referred to as contingencies;

therefore, the contract stipulates that the buyer will buy the home contingent upon A, B, and C. Although every contract will differ, we will discuss the three key contingencies common in almost all purchase contracts: Inspection, Appraisal, and Financing.

A) INSPECTION CONTINGENCY (DUE DILIGENCE PERIOD)

Majority of home purchases are contingent upon the buyers carrying out different investigations and inspections that are allowed within a particular, defined period. For instance, inspections are done within 10 days in Arizona. During this period, buyers can send a licensed home inspector and even other specialist licensed contractors to inspect the home and asses its current state. The buyers will consequently deliver the seller a notice of any objectionable issues and:

- Terminate the purchase

- Allows the seller to repair the objected areas

- Opt to proceed with the purchase and assume the property at its current state

In Arizona, just like it's the case in other states, the buyer can cancel merely on grounds of change of heart. There is no set-out standard based on which to determine the sufficiency of the buyer's reason to cancel. You can significantly minimize the likelihood of a buyer canceling during the inspection period by:

- Gauging motivation. The level of motivation will translate to how the buyer accepts the home.

- Conducting a home inspection before listing your home and ensure you repair the areas discovered by the inspector.

- Revealing to the buyer all identifiable negative aspects of the home prior to signing the contract. This reduces the likelihood of canceling following the admission of those items and also eliminates these items as areas of negotiation for any items that you are not willing to repair e.g. an aging roof that needs replacement and you don't want to replace it yourself. Disclosing such information in prior will reduce the likelihood of the buyer trying to negotiate a lower price or demanding a roof replacement due to the aged roof.

- Reducing the inspection period. You can settle with the buyers to a seven-day inspection period instead of the common 10 or more days.

- No doesn't mean the deal is completely dead. If a buyer cancels after discovering some conditions through inspection, disclose your readiness to address their concerns and they are likely to continue with the negation process.

- Issuing a home warranty. If still pending, propose a home warranty to cater for some of the buyer's greater worries as is the case with old but functioning items such as old air conditioner. Covering such old items will help see the deal through should they fail in future.

B) APPRAISAL CONTINGENCY

Every conventional bank will demand that your buyer get an appraisal from an unbiased third party. The appraiser provides an evaluation of the value and guarantees the bank that the home is not overpriced. In most cases, appraised values tend to match the purchase price. When the appraised value exceeds the purchase price, there are no changes and the buyer proceeds with the purchase. On the other hand, if the appraised value falls below the purchase price, the buyer can opt to exit the contract. It is very difficult to predict and overcome low appraisals, but the following tips will help you overcome this problem:

- Request the buyer to waive the appraisal contingency. Although it's a big request, very high demand homes or multiple offers can help you ensure the buyer waives his right to cancel following a low appraisal.

- Ensure your agent issues the appraiser with similar sales that rationalize your price or else appraisal will be an issue.

- Request for a quick appraisal. Discuss with your buyer so that an appraisal is ordered quickly to ensure you are able to address low appraisal right away and avoid being stunned late in the process.

- Issue the appraiser with a list of all upgrades undertaken in the home during the past five years. This will ensure all upgrades are considered and rank your home higher in the market.

- When the appraisal is low, negotiate with the buyer to meet you halfway or make up the difference. Don't rule out a deal due to a low appraisal. Offer to lower the price by half of the difference and request the buyers to come with more cash to cover the other half if they have extra cash to cover the difference between the purchase price and the appraised value.

c) ABILITY TO OBTAIN FINANCING

In any case, your buyer has to acquire the funds to buy your home. There are varying ways to source funds such as cash purchase and buyers selling their valuables to purchase your home. Regardless of the type of financing, the following tips can help you ensure the buyer doesn't fail to come with money as the deal closes.

Request the potential buyer to submit a verified pre-qualification form issued by the intended lender to prove qualification for a loan. Although most lenders are exhaustive when qualifying buyers to rule out adverse financial situations, you should not fully depend on the lender to qualify your home buyer.

Below are some questions that you can ask your buyers lender:

- In case the appraisal is low, does the buyer have sufficient cash to cover the difference?

- Did the lender evaluate the buyer's credit? How is the credit history?

- Does the buyer have sufficient funds to cover the down payment and closing costs or will they be borrowing or saving for it?

- Is the borrower a regular employee or self-employed? It is a requirement to submit two years tax returns for the loans. Did the borrower submit them or give the lender their word?

- Is the prospective buyer selling their current home?

- Was desktop underwriter used to pre-qualify the buyer? If not, why not? The system ensures minimal risks of financial issues in future.

- Did any concerns arise when financing this buyer?

- For how long has your institution been lending and how many loans do you finance in a year? More seasoned lenders guarantee a smooth process.

D) Cash

Cash is the best option from a financing viewpoint since buyers are not dependent on a lending institution to qualify them to purchase your home. However, not all cash offers are the same and you should examine some key details.

- Request for proof of funds so as to ascertain that the buyer actually has the money. This can be a letter signed and dated by the buyer's bank manager, investment adviser, or other official documents indicating the genuine possession of the necessary funds.

- For accounts that are under the names of another person or a business, get a signed letter from the account owner clarifying in the availability of the funds and allowing the buyer to utilize them as they please.

- Is the buyer still receiving an appraisal? If the contract fails to stipulate that the buyer is not using the appraisal contingency, it could still be included in the contract. Ensure you make this clear. Have faith in your agent and his/her advice too.

Although you can never be certain that your prospective home buyer will complete the purchase of your home; adhering to the above guidelines will significantly increase the chances of a successful process. Every contract has unique distinctions and precise details that a professional will help you analyze one by one. With the expertise of a professional agent, you will quickly finalize the sale of your home and sell it only once!

CHAPTER 12

EFFECTIVENESS OF INTERNET BASED MARKETING

STUDIES CONDUCTED ON four real estate websites, namely Redfin, Trulia (TRLA), Zillow (Z), and Realtor.com showed that they attract 61 million visitors of the 67 million real estate website traffic in the U.S per month. This sizable traffic to the above-named websites has translated hundreds of millions in revenue and has completely transformed the real estate sales sector. Buyers are now more enticed to look up properties on the Internet rather than physically visiting random open houses. A study conducted by the National Association of Realtors showed that Ninety percent of the property buyers begin their journey on the Internet before finally going to see the property physically.

Zillow, Redfin, and Trulia said they haven't done away with their real estate brokers when interviewed by Bloomberg Business Weekly on March 7, 2013. The founder of Stunning Home Realty started the company in 2013 after working for another firm for 6 years. The Internet was fast changing the market and the company he was working for had failed to adapt to this new trend. When Stunning Homes was launched it began with only one assistant.

He later brought in more agents to improve the company's sales necessary for growing the business. Stunning Homes Realty has always selected talented and goal oriented professionals in a bid to boost its business and provide buyers with the best solutions.

Most local companies in the Phoenix area had not recognized the power the Internet wields. We noted that having a strong Internet presence would translate to more sales. The company took advantage of this window and now thanks to SEO (Search Engine Optimization), we are listed on Google results' first page for searches involving properties in Chandler, Gilbert, Tempe, and other nearby cities by owning the domains ChandlerHomes.com, GilbertHomes.com, and TempeHomes.com.

I have always welcomed new marketing strategies and encourage the team to experiment with new tactics. We have gained quite a following on the Internet and today I get invited to speak at real estate seminars and conferences about focusing on Internet marketing. Stunning Homes Realty has been lauded for its early Internet marketing initiative and has attracted a huge following from players in the real estate industry.

What people want to know is how we implemented our strategies and, the answer is, we select talented professionals to help our company meet its objectives. My team plays an integral role in helping boost our digital footprint, and I support them financially. Financial support is key and makes a difference in the long run. Zillow recently purchased Trulia in a bid to strengthen their market share in the real estate on the Internet. This can be seen as creating a monopoly by offering two diverse real estate brands. This move strengthens their web presence and reduces unhealthy competition.

We spoke to a Pro Broker Trulia and a Premier Broker on Zillow about how their company takes advantage of its web presence and their dominance. Among the things they had to say, is that the company takes advantage of the Pay Per Click (PPC) program that increases traffic to their website and ultimately increases revenue generation. Their lead coordination system now has thousands of entries in their database.

By identifying that people today read less and watch more, videos are playing a great role when it comes to online marketing. We have a team of professionals creating informative videos and custom content for our inventory. One of our leading podcast website namely,

Our intensive Internet campaign and presence has resulted in more sales and better brand recognition. Our conversion rate is impressive, and we sell our inventory much faster and at a great price too. We have been number 1 on most Search Engines for properties many of the neighborhoods we operate in. We pride ourselves on having the best and most successful real estate agents in the city. Having a team of professionals who identify the Internet as a powerful tool is also key to the success of the business.

Embracing the Internet as a marketing tool and focusing information sharing has helped us transform our business. On the Internet, you are addressing a worldwide audience hungry for information and this, in the long run, translates to more sales. Today, potential buyers will first research about a product on the Internet before paying attention to other media.

Chapter 13

Your Next Step

Thank you for taking the time to read this book. I hope that you received tremendous value from these pages. There are a lot of things to consider when buying a home. Don't let it overwhelm you!

Please call me directly on my cell at 480-266-9960 or visit my website at www.stevetrang.com to find out how we can help you sell your home faster, for more money, and with less hassle while delivering 5-star service.

About The Author

STEVE TRANG IS the broker and owner of Stunning Homes Realty. When he founded the company, Steve knew he wanted to change the home selling experience. Selling a home for most people will be one of the most stressful events in their lives.

His purpose is to remove the stress and make each and every client's experience as smooth as possible. Steve does this by providing the highest quality of customer service from the initial phone call and consultation, throughout the selling process, and for years after the sale.

www.ingramcontent.com/pod-product-compliance
Lightning Source LLC
LaVergne TN
LVHW011430080426
835512LV00005B/362